Rain Forest Animals

by Nancy Leber

Reading Consultant: Wiley Blevins, M.A.
Phonics/

Compass Point Books
3109 West 50th Street, #115
Minneapolis, MN 55410

Visit Compass Point Books on the Internet at *www.compasspointbooks.com*
or e-mail your request to *custserv@compasspointbooks.com*

Photographs ©: Cover and p. 1: Bruce Coleman, Inc./Byron Jorjorian, p. 6: Minden
Pictures/Michael and Patricia Fogden, p. 7 (left): Bruce Coleman, Inc./Michael and Patricia
Fogden, p. 7 (right): Minden Pictures/Michael and Patricia Fogden, p. 8: Minden
Pictures/Michael and Patricia Fogden, p. 9: Minden Pictures/Frans Lanting, p. 10: Minden
Pictures/Frans Lanting, p. 11: Bruce Coleman, Inc./Kike Calvo V.W., p. 12: Corbis/Michael and
Patricia Fogden

Editorial Development: Alice Dickstein, Alice Boynton
Photo Researcher: Wanda Winch
Design/Page Production: Silver Editions, Inc.

Library of Congress Cataloging-in-Publication Data
Leber, Nancy.
 Rain forest animals / by Nancy Leber.
  p. cm. — (Compass Point phonics readers)
 Summary: Presents the different activities of a variety of rain forest
animals by day and by night, in a text that incorporates phonics
instruction and rebuses.
 Includes bibliographical references (p. 16).
 ISBN 0-7565-0523-2 (hardcover : alk. paper)
 1. Rain forest animals—Juvenile literature. 2. Reading—Phonetic
method—Juvenile literature. [1. Rain forest animals. 2. Animals. 3.
Rebuses. 4. Reading—Phonetic method.] I. Title. II. Series.
 QL112.L43 2003
 591.734—dc21   2003006368

Table of Contents

Dear Parent or Caregiver,

Welcome to Compass Point Phonics Readers, books of information for young children. Each book concentrates on specific phonic sounds and words commonly found in beginning reading materials. Featuring eye-catching photographs, every book explores a single science or social studies concept that is sure to grab a child's interest.

So snuggle up with your child, and let's begin. Start by reading aloud the Mother Goose nursery rhyme on the next page. As you read, stress the words in dark type. These are the words that contain the phonic sounds featured in this book. After several readings, pause before the rhyming words, and let your child chime in.

Now let's read *Rain Forest Animals*. If your child is a beginning reader, have him or her first read it silently. Then ask your child to read it aloud. For children who are not yet reading, read the book aloud as you run your finger under the words. Ask your child to imitate, or "echo," what he or she has just heard.

Discussing the book's content with your child:
Explain to your child that there are rain forests all over the world. Many animals live in rain forests. They depend on the trees to live in and sleep in, for protection, and for food such as leaves and fruit. Orangutans are huge apes that live in trees, as monkeys do. Jaguars often nap in trees.

At the back of the book is a fun Concentration game. Your child will take pride in demonstrating his or her mastery of the phonic sounds and the high-frequency words.

Enjoy Compass Point Phonics Readers and watch your child read and learn!

One, Two, Three

One, two, three, four, **five,**
Once **I** caught a fish **alive,**
Six, seven, eight, **nine,** ten,
But **I** let it go again.
Why did you let it go?
Because it bit **my** finger so.
Which finger did it **bite?**
The little one upon the **right.**

What is green, wet, and hot?
A rain forest!
Rain falls every day.
Rain helps trees and plants grow.

A rain forest has many kinds of wild animals.

Let us read about what they do in the daytime and the nighttime.

In the daytime, monkeys go up high.
They chit chat as they play.
At night, they quiet down and sleep.

In the daytime, giant apes eat
plants and fruit.
At night, they make beds of leaves.
Some of the leaves are huge.

In the daytime, the crocodile rests on dry land.
At night, it takes a swim.
It might find fish to eat.

The  jaguar is a big cat.
In the daytime, it rests and sleeps.
At night, it hunts in the dark.
It creeps up on small animals.

In the daytime, bats sleep
upside down.
At night, they wake up to eat.
The bats find fruit or bugs. Yum!

Word List

Long _i_ (_i, igh, y_)

_i_
find
giant
kinds
quiet
wild

igh
high
might
night

_y_
dry

Soft _g_
giant
huge

High-Frequency
down
every
falls
some

Science
animals
dark
rain forest

Concentration

You will need:
- 16 game pieces, such as pennies or checkers

high

dry

find

wild

night

find

down

wild

14

How to Play

- Cover the words with the game pieces. Players take turns uncovering one word and reading it, then uncovering another word and reading it. If the 2 words are the same, the player takes the game pieces. If the 2 words are not the same, the player covers them with the game pieces, and the next player goes.
- Play until all word pairs have been uncovered. The player with the most game pieces wins.

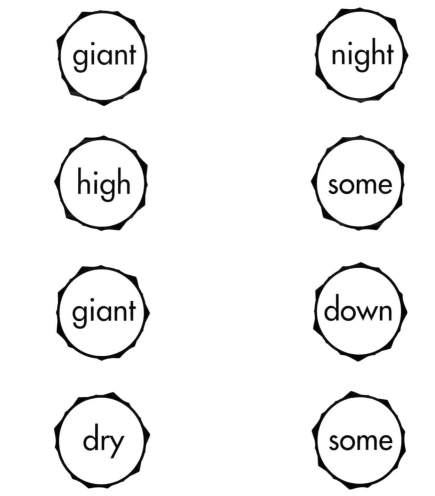

Read More

Frost, Helen. *Jaguars*. Rain Forest Animals Series. Mankato, Minn.: Pebble Books, 2002.

Galko, Francine. *Rain Forest Animals*. Animals in Their Habitats Series. Chicago, Ill.: Heinemann Library, 2002.

Longnecker, Theresa. *Who Grows Up in a Rain Forest? A Book About Rain Forest Animals and Their Offspring*. Minneapolis, Minn.: Picture Window Books, 2003.

Whitehouse, Patricia. *Hiding in a Rain Forest*. Animal Camouflage Series. Chicago, Ill.: Heinemann Library, 2003.

Index